This book belongs to

a Paul Doodles original

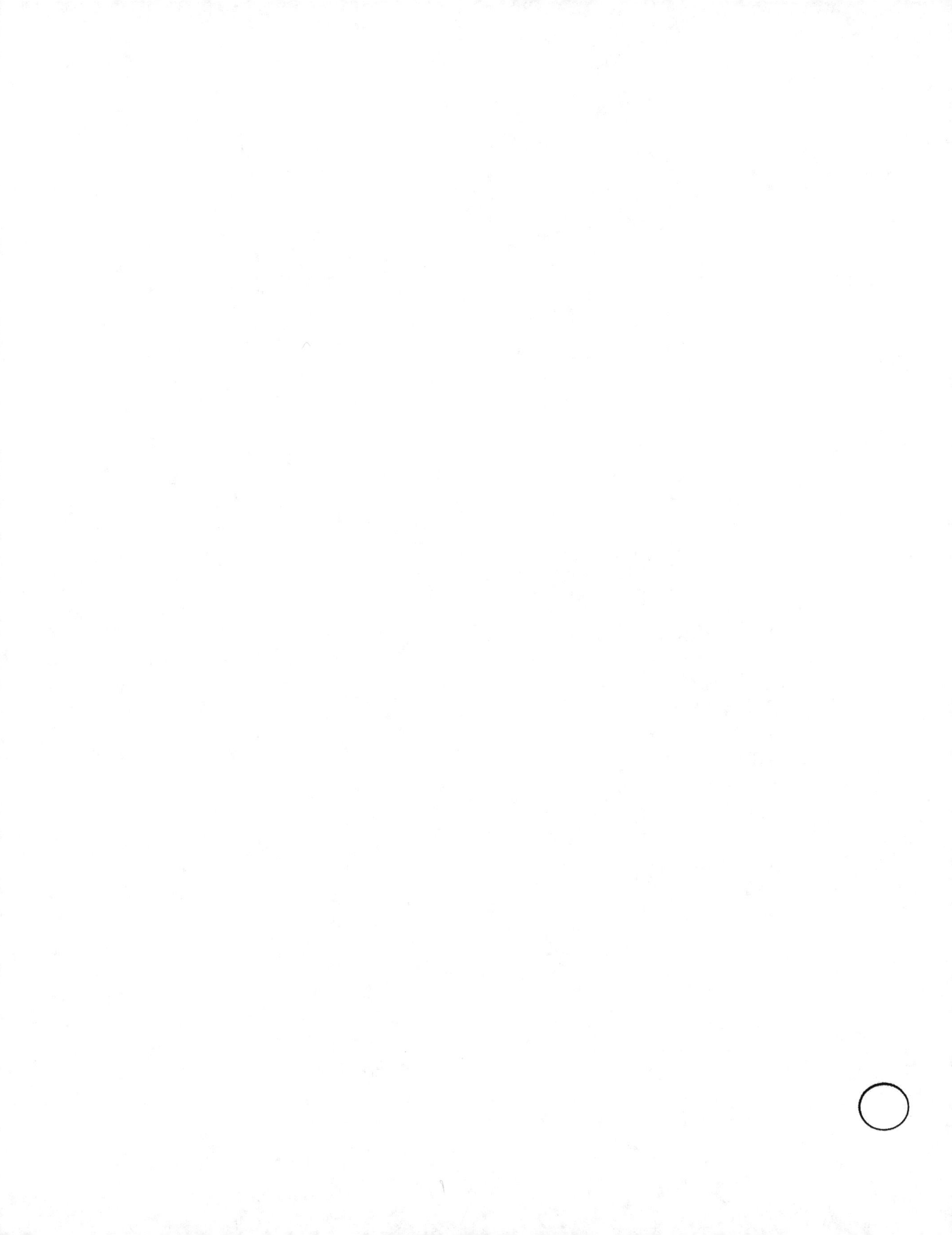

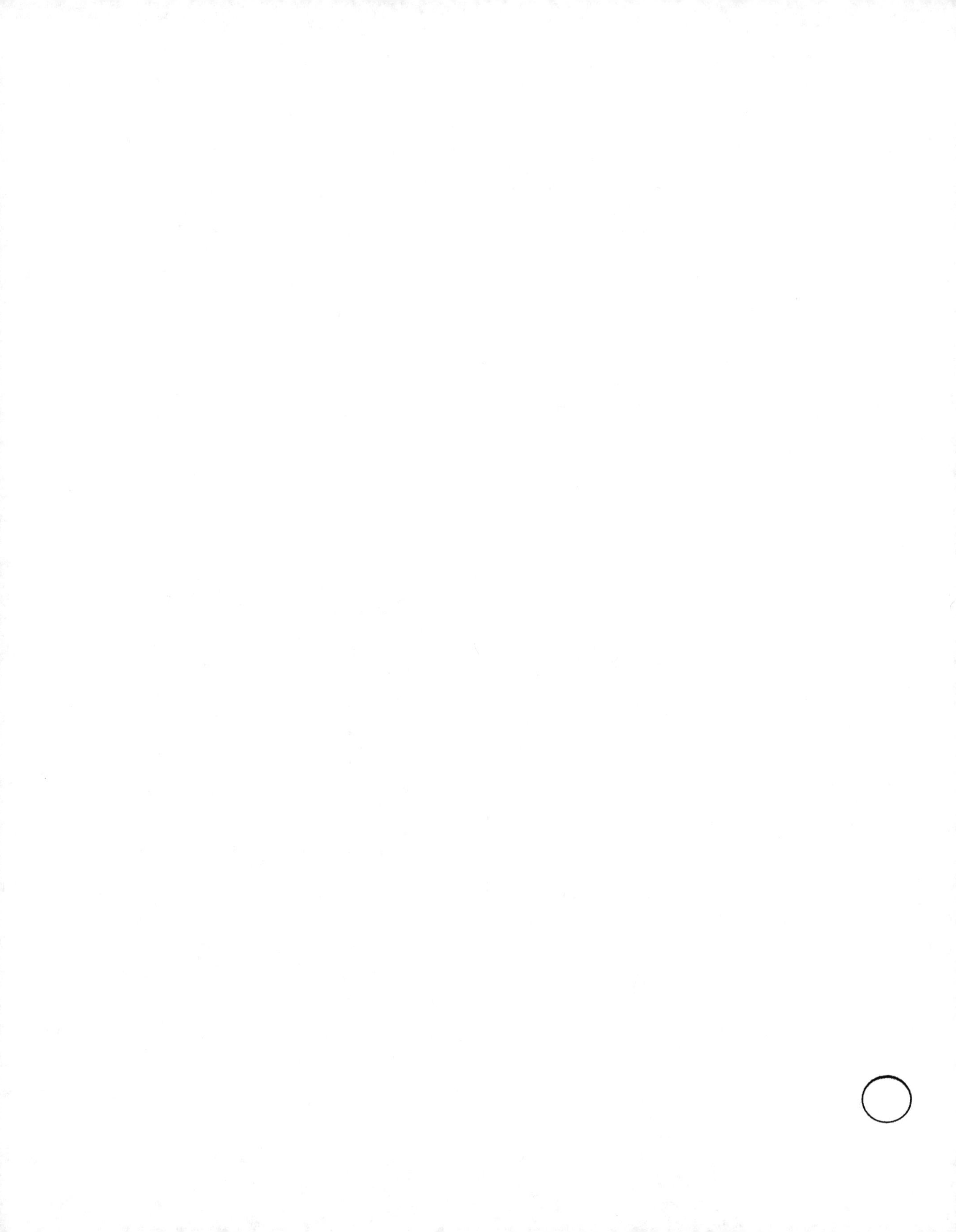

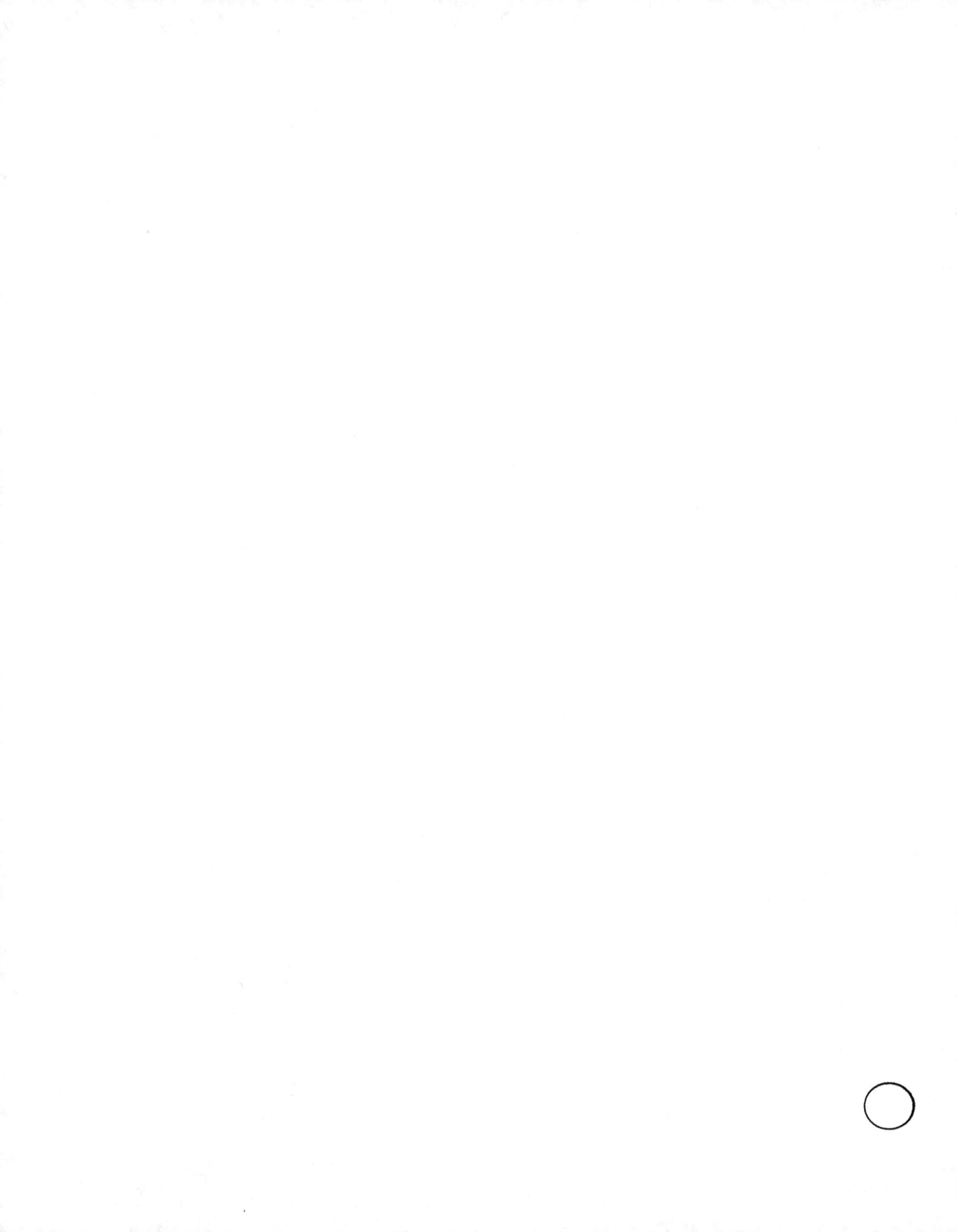

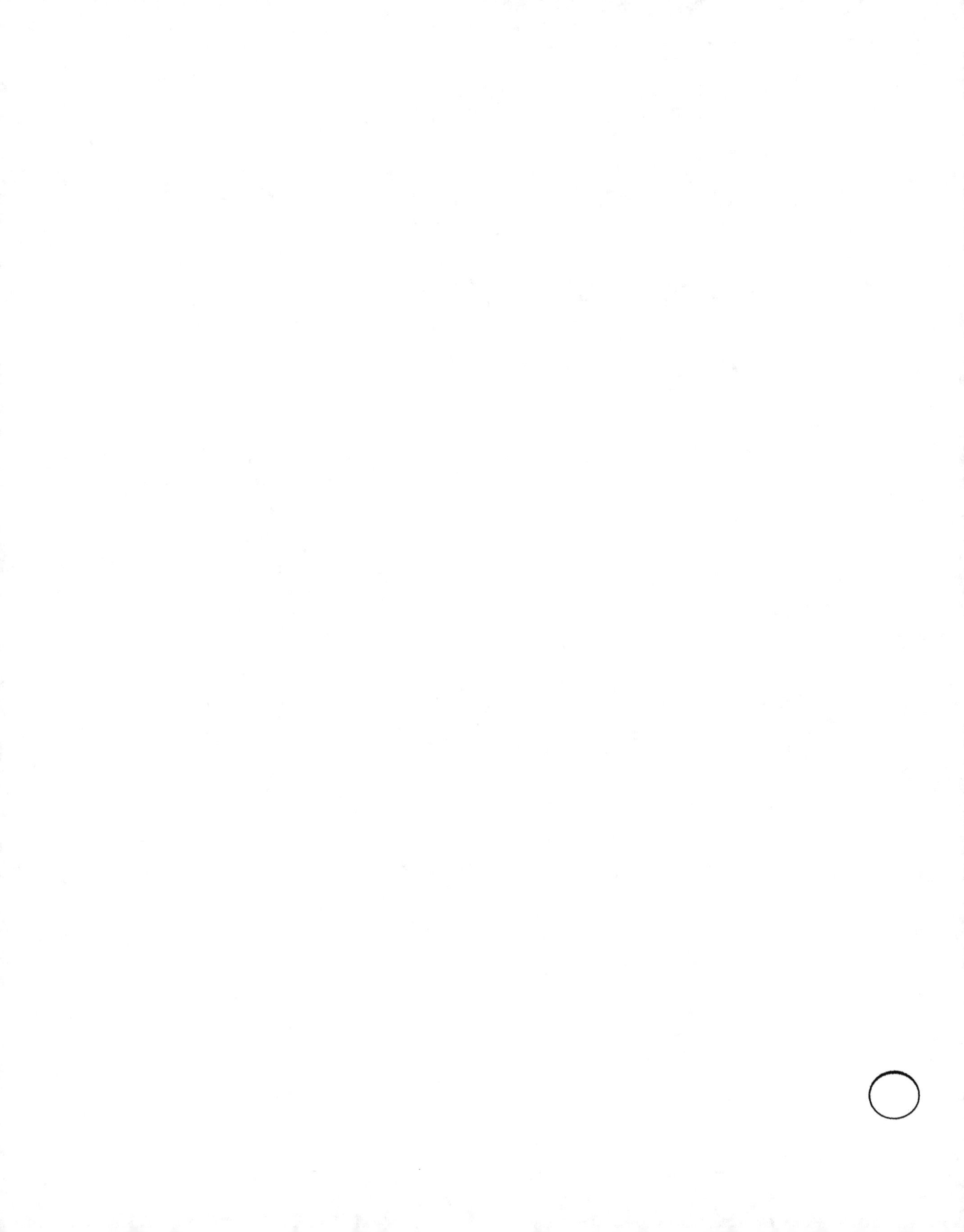

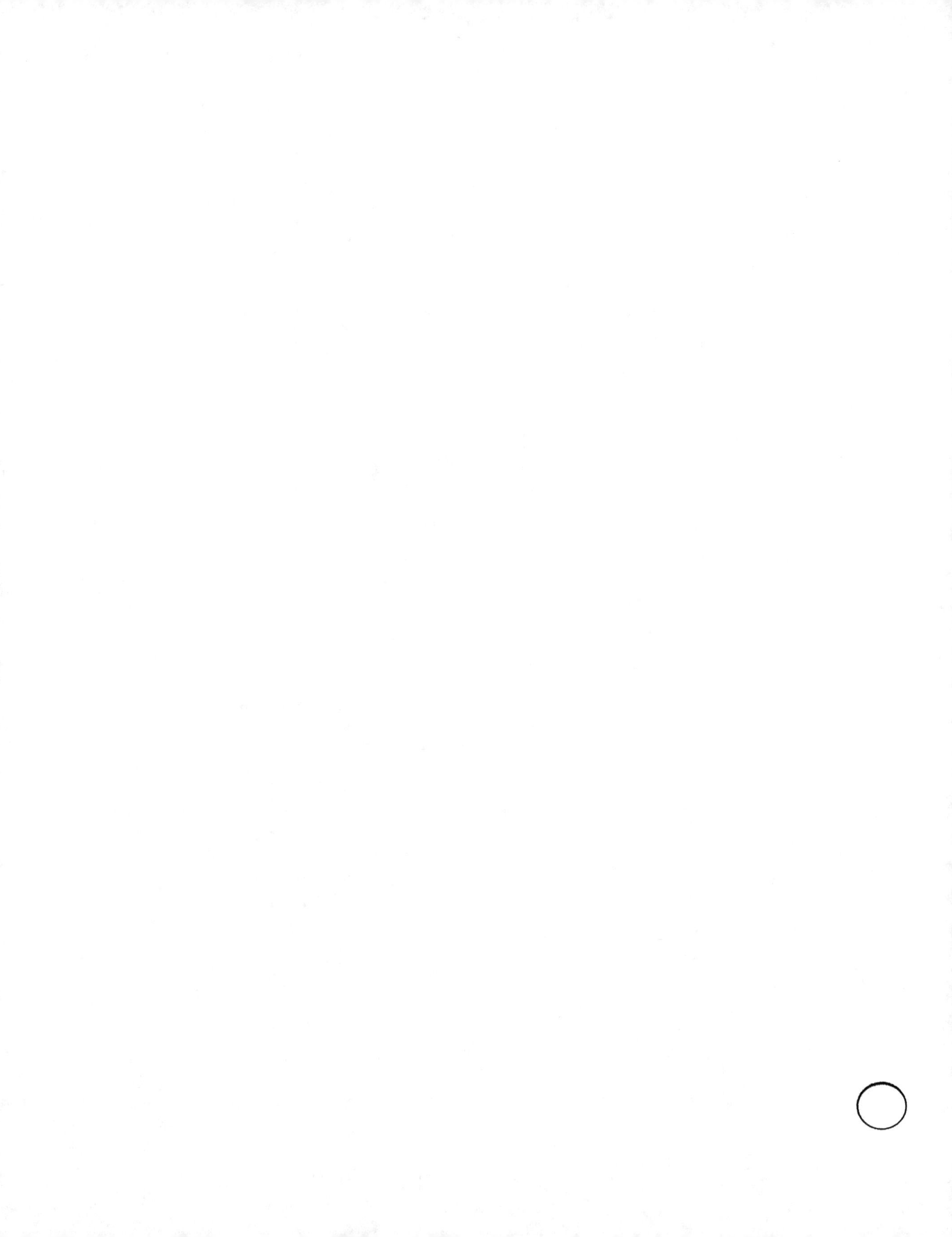

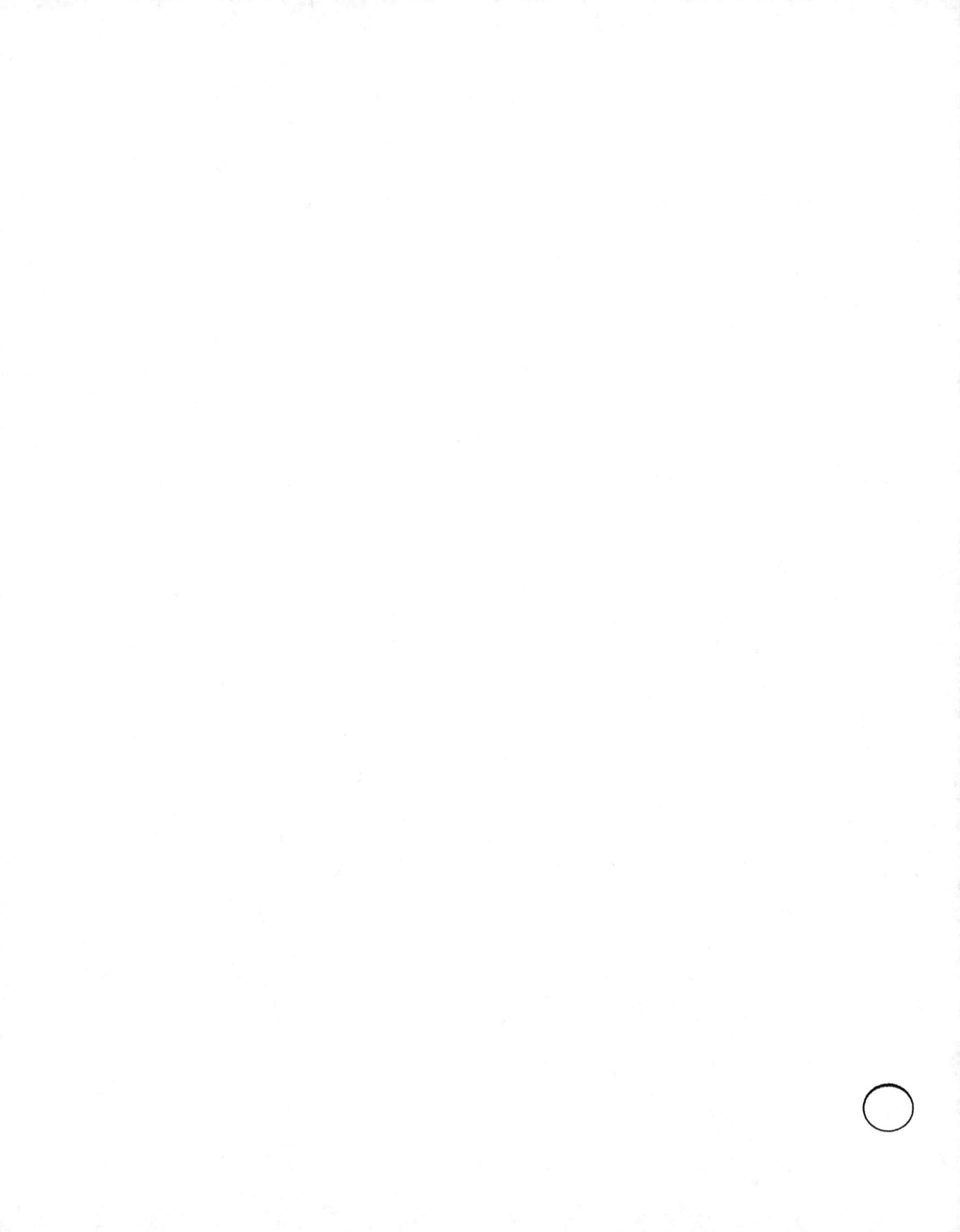

Time to get a new notebook